Modern Praise for
Foretold

"The research Bob has done for Foretold is fascinating, the findings throughout the entire project are an interesting and thought-provoking catalyst to sharing the gospel…"

Josh Walsh
Co-executive Producer, *I Can Only Imagine*
Co-Producer, *I Still Believe*

"The value of a tool like Foretold should never be underestimated in our scientific age where people need to see things for themselves. This resource lets users empirically verify the truth that God has left in Scripture, and a history that points to Him!

The overwhelming prophetic evidence of God's fingerprints in History is an important reminder that we should not be so skeptical about what His Word teaches. I highly recommend this powerful witnessing tool!"

Dr. David Geisler
President, Norm Geisler International Ministries

"I think Foretold is desperately needed. There is no better way to draw eyes to this property than through professional, Hollywood CGI and Visual Effects and our team at CAMd is ready to pounce on this amazing concept and see it come to life!"

Scott Smith
Academy Award Winning Visual FX Supervisor

"As one who reads in the Bible almost every day and also one who loves history, I find this book compelling and fascinating. This book has the opportunity to convince many skeptics all for the good of the Kingdom. I pray for terrific distribution and many to have their faith challenged and confirmed."

Ron Blue
Founding Director, Kingdom Advisors

Praise from the Ancient Fathers for
Foretold

What effrontery were it to deny that, by these evidences, the authority of the prophets is established, the very thing being fulfilled to which they appeal in support of their credibility! "Behold, the former things are come to pass, and new things do I declare; before they spring forth I tell you of them," (Isaiah 42:9)...

...If the pious will duly meditate on these things, they will be sufficiently instructed to silence the cavils of the ungodly. The demonstration is too clear to be gainsaid.

John Calvin
Institutes of Christian Religion, 1.8.8,
circa 1539 A.D.

It should be particularly observed, with what eloquence and distinctness they foretell the greatest and most important matters, which are far removed from the scrutinizing research of every human and angelical mind, and which could not possibly be performed except by power Divine: Let it be noticed at the same time with what precision the predictions are answered by the periods that intervene between them, and by all their concomitant circumstances; and the whole world will be compelled to confess, that such things could not have been foreseen and foretold, except by an omniscient Deity.

James Arminius
The Works Of James Arminius,
Vol. 1, Oration III, The Certainty of Sacred Theology,
3. The Prophecies,
circa 1600 A.D.

ROBERT JACOBUS

FORETOLD
QuickShare Edition

Foretold, LLC
Ver 2.02

© 2016, © 2020 Foretold, LLC - A Pennsylvania Limited Liability Company

Print Paperback ISBN: 978-1-7347673-0-8
e-Book ePub ISBN: 978-1-7347673-1-5
Kindle Edition ISBN: 978-1-7347673-2-2

All rights reserved. No part of this book may be reproduced or transmitted in any form or by any means, electronic or mechanical, including photocopying, recording, or by an information storage and retrieval system - except by a reviewer who may quote brief passages in a review to be published for public or private consumption - without permission in writing from the publisher.

Every effort has been made by the author and publisher to ensure that the information contained in this book was correct as of press time. *Readers are encouraged to verify any information* contained in this book prior to taking any action on the information. Contact the publisher, Foretold, LLC, online at foretold.com or through email via publisher@foretold.com

THE HOLY BIBLE, NEW INTERNATIONAL VERSION®, NIV® Copyright © 1973, 1978, 1984, 2011 by Biblica, Inc.® Used by permission. All rights reserved worldwide.

Scripture taken from the New King James Version® is identified NKJV herein. Copyright © 1982 by Thomas Nelson. Used by permission. All rights reserved.

Endnotes and sources page 53.   Photo Credits see pages 54-55.

CAPTURE THE *Imagination!*

Predictions recorded 2,500 years ago about the destiny of 20 nations, city-states, races, and places can be tested and verified on film today.

END THE *Debate*

God uses history as His final, ever present, testimony to His existence and the authorship of His Book, the Holy Bible.

SEEING IS *Believing*

The predictions recorded in this Book can be measured and tested to show God authenticates His Word by writing history centuries before it happens.

The Nations FORETOLD

Over 2,000 Years Ago in the Holy Bible

- x Tyre
- Lebanon
- Samaria
- Philistines
  - Ashdod x
  - Ashkelon x
  - Gaza x
  - x Ekron
  - x Gath
- Ammon
- Moab
- Egypt
- x Memphis
- Israel
- Edom
- Jordan
- Egypt
- Saudi Arabia
- x Thebes

Seeing is Believing!

Modern Nations
X - Prediction Targets

The Age of the Bible
Predictions

Masoretic Text
- 1,000 Years Old -

Aleppo Codex - 950 AD

A series of Bible manuscripts produced by the family known as the Masoretes of Tiberias circa 895 AD to 950 AD.

Septuagint (LXX)
- 2,100 Years Old -

A Greek translation of the Hebrew Bible created 285-100 BC by a team of 70 scholars in Alexandria, Egypt.

Papyrus Rylands 458

THE FULL BIBLE WAS FOUND AMONG THE
DEAD SEA SCROLLS
- 2,100 YEARS OLD -

Every book from the Hebrew Bible (except Esther*) and fragments of the Greek Bible translation, the Septuagint, were found in the Quram Caves proving beyond a reasonable doubt the Tanahk (Old Testament) is over 2,100 years old.

Scroll Cave 4 of 11 - 250 BC

THE BIBLE IS ANCIENT BEYOND A
REASONABLE DOUBT

DIG DEEP
AGE OF THE BIBLE PREDICTIONS

THE HEBREW BIBLE is a collection of 24 books written over a 1,000 year period with the final books added sometime before 250-100 AD. Establishing the date of the predictions is crucial when testing the outcomes.

Claiming today (after it happened) to have foretold a historical event like the fall of the World Trade Center in 2001 is vastly different than pointing out the prediction in the New York Times from 1980. Predictions are writing history *before* it happens.

We know the predictions in the Tanakh (known as the Hebrew Bible and Christian Old Testament) are ancient beyond a reasonable doubt because of thousands of archaeological finds. These three are sufficient to end the debate:

FORETOLD AT LEAST 1000 YEARS AGO...

Masoretic Text - (895-950 AD) - A Jewish scholarly school in Palestine known as the Masoretes of Tiberias (500-1000 AD) produced the oldest dated manuscript called **Codex Cairensis** in 895 AD located today in Hebrew University, Jerusalem.

The Masoretes **Aleppo Codex** is housed at the Israel Museum in Jerusalem dated to 900-950 AD. Once a complete manuscript in Syria, approximately 200 pages (40%) of the codex were lost in transfer from Syria to Israel in the late 1940s and still the subject of search by collectors and the Mossad (Israel's CIA).

A third still later text dated 1008 AD, **Codex Leningradensis**, is housed in the Leningrad Public Library and testifies to being written by Aaron ben Moses ben Asher of the Masoretes family school.[1]

FORETOLD AT LEAST 2,100 YEARS AGO...

Septuagint - (250-100 BC) - The first five books of the Hebrew Bible, called the Pentateuch, were translated into Greek around 285-250 BC during the reign of Ptolemy II Philadelphus[2] with the remaining books in circulation by 100 BC.[3] A team of seventy scholars in Alexandria, Egypt labored to serve a Jewish community that only spoke Greek.[4]

The past century found Septuagint fragments among the 2,000 year old Dead Sea Scrolls giving final physical proof of the age of this Hebrew Bible translation.

NOW CONFIRMED, BEYOND A REASONABLE DOUBT...

Dead Sea Scrolls - (250-100 BC) - This library of scrolls was found in the 1940s and 1950s in 11 caves in and around Wadi Qumran west of the Dead Sea in modern Israel. The oldest text is a fragment of Exodus dating about 250 BC. An Isaiah Scroll dates from about 100 BC. Parts of every book of the Hebrew Bible and pieces of it's Greek translation, the Septuagint, were in the caves (except the book of Esther) meaning *the whole Hebrew Bible had to be completed 2,100 years ago.*[5]

Foretold

Edom

GPS:
30.3 LAT
35.4 LONG

Modern:
Jordan & Southern Israel

Prediction:
- Prophet Ezekiel - translation "God Strengthens"
- Date of Prediction - April 587 BC - April 586 BC
- Prediction - Ezekiel 35 - A Prophecy Against Edom (NIV)

[7] I will make Mount Seir a desolate waste and cut off from it all who come and go... [9] I will make you desolate forever; your towns will not be inhabited. Then you will know that I am the LORD.

Prediction:
- Prophet Jeremiah - translation "The Lord Throws"
- Date of Prediction - 626 BC - 586 BC
- Prediction - Chapter 49 - A Message About Edom (NIV)

...all its towns will be in ruins forever." ... [15] "Now I will make you small among the nations, despised among men. [16] The terror you inspire and the pride of your heart have deceived you, you who live in the clefts of the rocks, who occupy the heights of the hill. Though you build your nest as high as the eagle's, from there I will bring you down," declares the Lord ...

7

Edomite Lands

In Modern Jordan
Desolate

Dig Deep -
Edom Foretold

Resting mostly in what is now modern Jordan and south west Israel, Edom is historically traced in the Bible to be the progeny of Esau, brother of Jacob/Israel. Edom became an important Kingdom by the time of Assyrian power in the 8th century with its capital in Bozrah.

Edom appears to decline in the Babylonian advance of the 6th century BC. By the 4th century Nabateans traders from the east became culturally ascendant over any remaining Edomites. The Edomite name slowly disappears from history and the Nabatean culture, fired by trade routes and later, Hellenization, became ascendant by 300 BC.

The remaining Edomites (now known in Greek as Idumaeans) were attacked and slaughtered by the Jewish Maccabees in the 2nd century BC. The survivors were forced to be assimilated into Jewish culture.

By the fall of Jerusalem in 70 AD, the Edomites (Idumaeans) disappear from recorded history as a distinct people.

The now Nabatean culture grew prosperous in the heart of a great trading route, the King's Highway, through the 5th century AD. Yet, a curse was on the land (Malachi 1:2-5) and the civilization declined, last mentioned in burnt scrolls discovered in 1993 in a Petra Byzantine church dating to the end of the 6th century AD. [6]

The land was lost to the world by the 13th century AD only to be rediscovered centuries later in 1812. Again, skeptics who believed Edom legendary, were forced to see prophecy fulfilled again.

Edom

Today, Petra and the surrounding Edomite Cities are a wasteland save for a tourist trade visiting the vacant cities carved into the sides of the rocks.

Ruins Forever

FORETOLD EGYPT

GPS:
30 LAT
31 LONG
EGYPTIAN SINCE THE PHARAOHS

PREDICTION:
- Prophet Ezekiel - translation "God Strengthens"
- Date of Prediction - 587 BC
- Prediction - Chapter 29 - A Prophecy Against Egypt

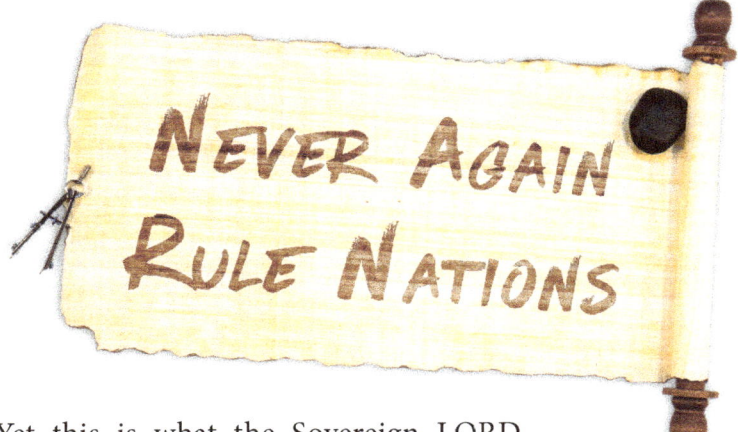

[13] "Yet this is what the Sovereign LORD says... There they will be a lowly kingdom. [15] It will be the lowliest of kingdoms and will never again exalt itself above the other nations. I will make it so weak that it will never again rule over the nations... (NIV)

1 1

Conquering Empire

In the shadow of former glory, modern Egypt remains a lowly kingdom with millions trapped in poverty.

to

Lowly Kingdom

Dig Deep -
Egypt Foretold

Information on this ancient empire dates back to 3,100 BC, over 5,000 years ago. 96% of Egypt today is desert with only 4% usable land. 99% of her present population lives in that 4% stretch along the Nile river.

The distance from other fertile (and populated) lands made for a natural desert barrier of protection from other cultures for most of her history. It was not so far that cultural interaction was prohibited, nor did it prevent her once vast armies from reaching out and ruling most of the known world.

Her present population is in direct descent from what we can best call the original Egyptians, the Naqada dating back to 3,000 BC.[7]

EGYPT — FORMER GLORY

At the time of Ezekiel's ministry of prediction, Egypt under Pharaoh Neco II had already faced rising Babylonian power on the field of battle suffering defeat in Carchemish in 605 BC and again in 601 BC with both sides suffering heavy losses. Jehoiakim, King of Judah rebelled against Babylon resulting in the capture of Jerusalem in 597 BC by Nebuchadnezzar while Neco II stayed neutral.

Rebellion in Babylon in 594 BC began to encourage western vassal kings (Judah's Zedekiah included) appointed by

Nebuchadnezzar to throw off Babylonian authority. Zedekiah ultimately did rebel with the hope of Egyptian help from Pharaoh Hophra. In 588 BC, Nebuchadnezzar invaded Judah and laid seige to Jerusalem. Hophra did march out to engage Babylonian forces but was repulsed and made a hasty retreat. Jerusalem was left alone and fell to utter destruction in 587 BC.[8]

Fulfillment:

Egypt, in one form or another, has existed since this prophecy was made in the 6th century BC. In 304 BC, Alexander the Great's Empire was being partitioned by his generals and Egypt fell to Ptolemy Lagos and remained under his dynasty for nearly three centuries. With the rise of the Roman Empire, Egypt became a province with rebuilding efforts focused on making the nation the unofficial Roman national granary.

After Roman Emperor Constantine granted freedom of worship to Christians in 313 AD, Egypt experienced a national conversion placing the nation slowly under Byantine power. In 619 AD, the Arabs invaded and after a series of defeats, Egypt became an Arab province under the Caliphs of Damascus. Political leaders converted to Islam followed by the gradual turn of the population.

From 835 AD to 1000 AD Egypt experienced a revival of it's economy and the founding of significant universities. Egypt's political history is difficult from this point forward as various Caliphs fought for power and the country faced difficult external military threats in the Fatimid period (969-1171 AD). Saladin united Egypt after the Crusaders attacked Cairo, eventually beating the Christian infidels back. This period of Ayyubid Rule lasted until 1250 AD giving way to the Mamluke Period till 1517 AD. The advance of the Ottoman Empire led to an era of neglectful Turkish control of Egypt.

The final centuries leading up to modern times involved French and British occupations with self-rule obtained at the close of WWII. At various points in history, Egypt regained power and beat back invading forces but the nation has never ruled over the other nations since Ezezkiel declared God's curse 2,500 years ago.

POLITICAL TURMOIL

EGYPT FULFILLED

After millennia of subjugation by foreign powers including the Macedonians, Arabs, Turks, and in modern times the French and British, Egypt remains a nation full of indigenous people dating back to the time of the Pharaohs.

EGYPT FULFILLED

A Lowly Nation

Economically Weak

1. Gross Domestic Product (GDP)*
   A. Egypt GDP = $236.5 Billion
   B. Israel GDP = $350.7 Billion
   C. USA GDP = $19.49 Trillion
   *official exchange rate

2. GDP per capita
   (annual household income)
   A. Egypt = $12,800 per year
   B. Israel = $36,400 per year
   C. USA = $59,800 per year

By virtually every measure Egypt remains third world.

2017 CIA Worldbook [9]

Never Rule Nations Again

Militarily Weak

Military Expenditures per Year
   A. Egypt Military 2017 = 1.42% GDP ($3.4 Bil)
   B. Israel Military 2017 = 4.43% GDP ($15.5 Bil)
   C. USA Military 2017 = 3.31% GDP ($645.2 Bil)

Egypt has not ruled the nations for 2,500 years.

2017 CIA Estimates [9]

FORETOLD: TYRE

GPS: 33.27 LAT   35.19 LONG
MODERN: SOUTHERN COASTAL LEBANON

PREDICTION:

- Prophet Ezekiel - name translates "God Strengthens"
- Date of Prediction - April 587 BC - April 586 BC
- Prediction - Chapter 26 - Prophecy Against Tyre

...³the Sovereign LORD says: I am against you, O Tyre, and I will bring many nations against you, like the sea casting up its waves. ⁴They will destroy the walls of Tyre and pull down her towers; I will scrape away her rubble and make her a bare rock. ⁵Out in the sea she will become a place to spread fishnets, for I have spoken, declares the Sovereign LORD. She will become plunder for the nations, ⁶ and her settlements on the mainland will be ravaged by the sword. Then they will know that I am the Lord...

¹²They [the nations] will plunder your wealth... and throw your stones, timber and rubble into the sea... ¹⁴ I will make you a bare rock, and you will become a place to spread fishnets. You will never be rebuilt, for I the LORD have spoken... (NIV)

Seafaring Superpower to Fishing Village

Dig Deep -
Tyre Foretold

In the present-day, Tyre, known as Sur in modern Lebanon, is a small town on a peninsula jutting into the Mediterranean from the mainland south of Beirut. The original city was built on an island roughly half a mile from the coast dating back to before 1400 BC.

Tyre became the region's dominate trading and maritime power by 1100 BC, planting colonies in Spain, Italy, and Africa. With Egypt's decline and extensive commerce with Israel, Tyre entered what some have called it's golden age in the 9th century BC. Tyre's primary trade was exporting glass and it's famous purple 'Tyrian' dyes.

The city-state grew as the natural layout made for excellent trading conditions. Ships docked with little threat from the ravages of the sea allowing goods to be taken by land or sea throughout the Middle East and beyond.

The key ingredient to Tyre's success was peace with surrounding nations to allow her mainland settlements and shipping industry to conduct commerce. Her long history included many treaties and ultimately the construction of a nearly impregnable fortress on the island to ward off marauders and nations seeking to spoil her vast wealth.

Plundered as a Sea Casting up its Waves (verses 3-6)

- 585 BC - For 13 years Tyre resisted as Nebuchadnezzar's armies utterly destroyed the mainland city but without a fleet, the island fortress remained.

- 332 BC - Alexander the Great conquered Tyre by building a bridge to the island.

- 315 BC - Destroyed again by one of Alexander's successors, former general, Antigonus.

- 219 BC - Antiochus III led the Seleucids to conquer Phoencia in war against the Ptolemies.

- 48 BC - Julius Caesar conquered and looted Tyre for it's wealth.

- 193 AD - Niger slaughtered many citizens and plundered Tyre during a struggle for Roman power.

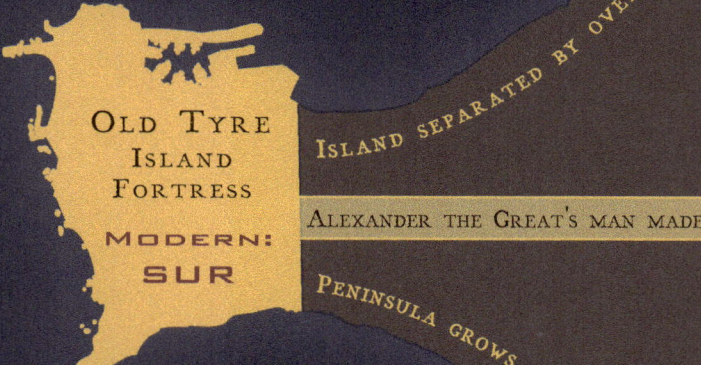

OLD TYRE ISLAND FORTRESS
MODERN: SUR

ISLAND SEPARATED BY OVER HALF MILE OF OCEAN

ALEXANDER THE GREAT'S MAN MADE BRIDGE

PENINSULA GROWS AROUND BRIDGE OVER CENTURIES

- 638 AD - Tyre was conquered by Arab Muslim forces.

- 1124 AD - Following the failure of his brother 14 years earlier, Baldwin II and the Crusaders accepted surrender of the starving Tyrians.

- 1291 AD - Muslims under Saladin massacred the population, sold the remaining into slavery, and destroyed everything stained by the touch of Christian infidels ruining the last vestiges of the great Tyrian trading Empire.[10]

 TYRE FORTRESS NEVER REBUILT (verses 12-14)

Today, Tyre, called Sur is a part of the nation of Lebanon near the border with Israel. It remains a small seaport town heavily reliant on the fishing trade.

Various rebel Islamic groups including the PLO, Hamas, and the Hezbollah guerrilla group allegedly base their operations out of southern Lebanon including Tyre. As a result, Israel occasionally pounds the area with artillery to minimize the terrorist threats.

Population is difficult to determine with the cazas (similar to a US county) of Tyr boasting 132,000 residents. Estimates put the inhabitants of Sur at 10,000-30,000 in 1996 according to the Association for Rural Development in Lebanon.

TYRE IMPOVERISHED FISHING VILLAGE (verse 5)

Association for Rural Development in Lebanon reports: The fishermen of Tyre and of Sarafand, grouped under one union, number 520 and use 215 small boats (the number of which has a tendency to increase every year). Of those, Tyre has about 300 fishermen and 170 small boats. Production stands at 275 tons of fish per year. The principal instruments of fishing are the multifilament net (2/3 of the fishing), and the fishing line (1/3 of the fishing).

90% of the fishing is done at night and utilizes small boats for an average of 180 days per year. The boats, generally between 8 to 10 meters, are well equipped and exploit the potentials offered by the actual fishing zones.

The port protects the boats well from the current, and has the necessary equipment except a dock for unloading. The income per fisherman is estimated at $200 USD per month. [11]

- Plundered by the Nations
- Fortress Never Rebuilt
- Fishing Village Today

-as Foretold

Lebanon

Tyre

Fishing Village

Fulfilled

Sea of Galilee

Israel

RAPID FIRE

PAGE 49

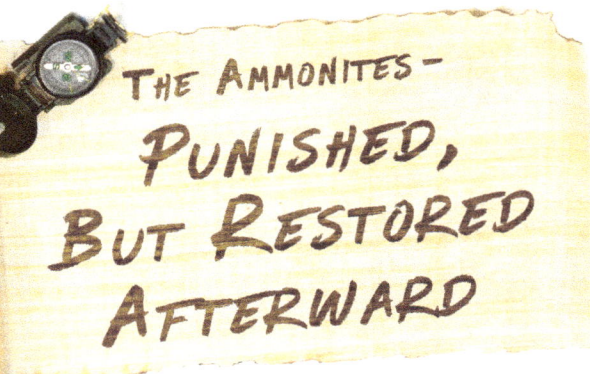

The Ammonites – Punished, But Restored Afterward

Ezekiel 25: 1-7 (circa 588 BC) - ... I will cut you off from the peoples, and I will cause you to perish from the countries; I will destroy you, and you shall know that I am the Lord.

Jeremiah 49: 1-6 (626-586 BC) - ...⁵ Behold, I will bring fear upon you," Says the Lord God of hosts, "From all those who are around you; You shall be driven out, everyone headlong, And no one will gather those who wander off. ⁶ But afterward I will bring back the captives of the people of Ammon," says the Lord. (NKJV)

LAND OF AMMON TODAY

The Ammonites were condemned by the Jewish prophets for their false religion and human sacrifice to their god, Molech.

After centuries of rivalry with the Israelites, the Ammonites slowly disappear from history after being defeated in the Jewish Maccabees wars.

Today, Amman, capital of Jordan, stands on the site of Rabbah, former chief city of the Ammonites with a 1.3 million population.

Rapid Fire

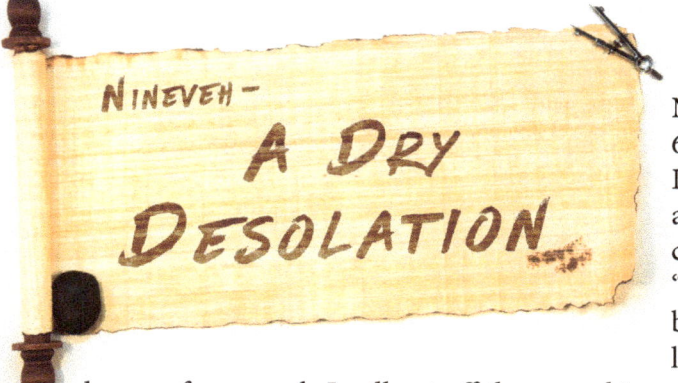

Nineveh – A Dry Desolation

Nahum 1 (663-612 BC) - [14] The Lord has given a command concerning you: "Your name shall be perpetuated no longer. Out of the house of your gods I will cut off the carved image and the molded image. I will dig your grave, for you are vile."

Zephaniah 2:13-15 (640-627 BC) - And He will stretch out His hand against the north, destroy Assyria, and make Nineveh a desolation, as dry as the wilderness. (NKJV)

Nineveh Today

Nineveh was unequalled in size by all other ancient cities with walls 100 feet high and 50 feet thick. Three chariots could ride abreast on top of the walls.

The combined armies of Babylon and Medes attacked Assyria beginning in 614 BC and sacked the capital Nineveh in 612 BC reducing the city to a pile of debris.

Assyria passed into the pages of history with her massive carved images buried in the earth.

RAPID FIRE

The Philistines – Damned to Extinction

Amos 1:7-8
(760 - 750 BC)
...I will send a fire upon the wall of Gaza, Which shall devour its palaces.

⁸ I will cut off the inhabitant from Ashdod,
And the one who holds the scepter from Ashkelon;
I will turn My hand against Ekron,
And the remnant of the Philistines shall perish,"
Says the Lord God. (NKJV)

Philistines Today

The beginning of the end for the Philistines was around the time of the fall of Assyria and the rise of Babylonian Empire in the latter part of the 7th century.

The Philistines joined Egypt in an anti-Babylonian alliance that was doomed to failure. Nebuchadnezzar burned the cities, slaughtered the inhabitants, and ultimately deported the remaining populace of Philista ending the political and cultural existence of the Philistines by 603 BC.

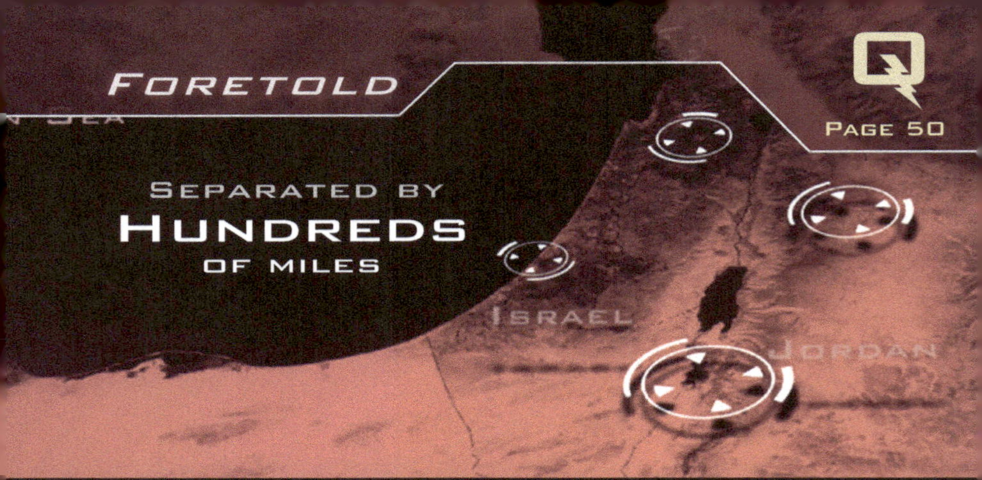

Foretold

Q
PAGE 50

SEPARATED BY
HUNDREDS
OF MILES

OVER
THOUSANDS
OF YEARS

SPANNING
MILLIONS
OF LIVES

PREDICTIONS PROVE GOD INSPIRED THE BIBLE
WITH PRECISION BEYOND A REASONABLE DOUBT

COMBINING THE DATA OF THE NATIONS, RACES, & PLACES TARGETED BY A BIBLE PREDICTION

HUNDREDS OF MILES

The distance between each site targeted by a Bible prediction is difficult to understand in an age of planes, trains, and automobiles. Modern engines have turned hundreds of miles from months into hours of travel.

Each location targeted by a prediction was often months of hard travel apart. In the time of the Bible, a trip by foot or on horse and camel would take months, if not years, to reach just three or four of the locations foretold by just a single prophet like Ezekiel.

THOUSANDS OF YEARS

The length of time that has passed between the predictions and today makes the impact of their accuracy all the more devastating.

Libraries across the earth contain pieces, full copies and translations of the Bible demanding an age going back thousands of years. Yet, no matter how late you date the creation of the Bible, the miracles stand.

Throughout seasons, wars, the rise and fall of empires, and the passing of far more than 40 generations, the predictions prevail far more than 1,500 years through today - as foretold.

MILLIONS OF LIVES

While we can only make educated guesses as to the populations of ancient empires, we know that if each generation averaged only 50,000 people till today, over 2 million lives would have come and gone. Most of the six nations considered here were far larger driving the total population well past 12 million souls over the march of time - each as foretold.

TRILLIONS OF VARIABLES

Each individual, each family, each clan & tribe make a myriad of decisions that can change the course of history over the centuries. Innovations, invention, disease, conflict, natural disasters, invasion - all shape the future making predicting just one life improbable, a nation impossible, but accurately predicting six nations, races and places reveals the Bible was written through the very Hand of God -

BEYOND A REASONABLE DOUBT

God Authenticates His Word

By Writing History BEFORE It Happens.

"Extraordinary Claims require Extraordinary Evidence"
- David Hume (1748) to Carl Sagan (1980)

Believers lack modern, testable evidence for many of the fantastic miracles recorded in the Bible.

Thus, to discredit the Bible, Enlightenment philosophers and scientists from David Hume, through Pierre-Simon Laplace, to contemporary Carl Sagan, seized upon this with the axiom *"Extraordinary claims require extraordinary evidence"*.

Done. God embedded evidence that transcends time and space to corroborate the otherwise absurd, supernatural Bible stories.

By testing ancient predictions against the march of history and modern observations, we have collected extraordinary evidence that perpetually stands as proof beyond a reasonable doubt.

The predictions about these nations, races and places represent millions of lives, spread over thousands of years, separated by hundreds of miles - all with a variety of different outcomes accurately foretold again, and again.

Because the Bible accurately foretold detailed predictions thousands of years ago in the face of trillions of variables, we can logically correlate that God has supernaturally protected *every word* of the Bible - including the verses with no direct evidence (from the verses we like to the difficult ones we don't).

> *The same God* who accurately damned the Philistines to extinction is *the same God* who records a world wide flood.
>
> *The same God* who said Edom would stand desolate forever is *the same God* who claims to have parted the Red Sea.
>
> *The same God* who permanently cursed Egypt to weakness, is *the same God* who lead millions of Israelites with a giant pillar of fire.

The predictive verses we can test and miracles we can see prove the Bible true. What we can prove allows us the intellectual certainty, or faith, to believe the Bible verses we can not.

Our Extraordinary Evidence -
Miracles Captured On Camera

The Bible is...

✡ A Library of Hebrew Scrolls

The Bible is a collection of 24 scrolls called the Tanakh (Hebrew Bible) falling into three divisions, the Law, the Prophets, and the Writings, inspired by the God of Israel.

Often called the *Kitvei Hakodesh* (the Holy Writings), the Hebrew Bible is divided into 39 books in the Old Testament of the Christian Bible which adds the Gospels of Jesus Christ and Apostolic Letters (New Testament).

Our purpose here is simply to test the predictions in the Hebrew Bible to establish if it's claim to Divine authorship is true.

✡ Written over 1,000 Years

Exodus	Judges	Kings Begin	Nation Divides		Israel Falls	Judah Falls	Nation Returns
Torah			Psalms		Amos		Daniel / Malachi
1450 BC	1200 BC	1000 BC		800 BC	Isaiah 600 BC Ezekiel Jeremiah		400 BC

The writing of the Bible is traditionally recorded to have begun through the hand of Moses after the Exodus of the Jews from slavery in Egypt. Named and unnamed prophets added books as the centuries of punishment and restoration past for the Israeli nation. The Jewish Prophets recorded history, defined right from wrong, called citizens to repent, and predicted the future throughout a 1,000 year period from 1450 BC to 400 BC.

✡ By over 30 Authors

No political, religious, or wealth class had exclusive dominance over the creation and preservation of the Hebrew Bible.

Prophets great and small, often credentialed by supernatural predictions or miraculous acts, wrote history, proclaimed right from wrong, and foretold the future.

✡ Across Hundreds of Miles

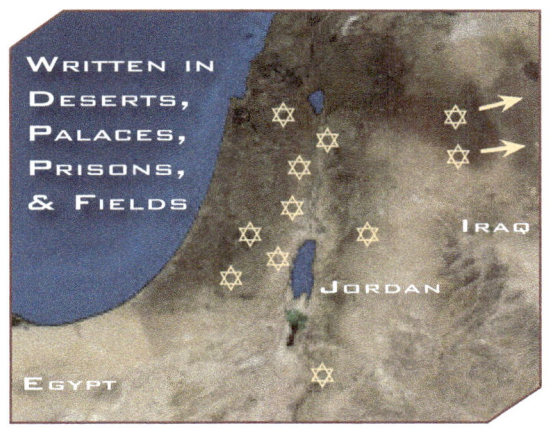

Various prophets wrote in times of war, in times of peace, from jail, while captive in foreign countries, and in palaces - separated by centuries and journeys that would take months if not years to complete.

...Over 28% Prediction [12]

Why This Matters...

The men who began the work of writing the Holy Bible were made keenly aware of the need for evidence that would persuade over the millennia.

Directly empowered and inspired by God, these men authenticated the Scriptures by writing history centuries and millennia before it happened.

Proof You Need

(Isaiah 41 - NIV) [21]"Present your case," says the LORD ."Set forth your arguments," says Jacob's King. [22]*"Bring in your idols to tell us what is going to happen... declare to us the things to come,* [23] *tell us what the future holds, so we may know that you are gods...*

One of the authors of the Bible, the prophet Isaiah (700 B.C.), debated the unbelievers of his day with this challenge - predict the future and we will know you speak for God.

(Isaiah 46 - NIV) [9] Remember the former things, those of long ago; I am God, and there is no other; I am God, and there is none like me. [10] *I make known the end from the beginning, from ancient times, what is still to come...*

(Isaiah 48 - NIV) [3] *I foretold the former things long ago, my mouth announced them and I made them known; then suddenly I acted, and they came to pass.* [4] *For I knew how stubborn you were; the sinews of your neck were iron, your forehead was bronze.* [5] *Therefore I told you these things long ago; before they happened I announced them to you so that you could not say, 'My idols did them; my wooden image and metal god ordained them.'* [italicized emphasis added]

Reveals Right from Wrong

After rescuing the Hebrew race from slavery in Egypt around 1440 BC by several supernatural interventions (plagues, parting the Red Sea, etc), God gave the 10 Commandments and various national & personal laws to define right from wrong (sin), how people are to behave, and order society.

Sin is missing the mark of anything less than perfect obedience to His laws.

...What God Wants

I am the Lord,
have no other gods before me

Do not make a Carved Image

Do not carry the name of
the Lord your God in vain

Do not work on the Sabbath,
keep it holy for the Lord

Honor your Father and Mother

You shall not Murder

You shall not commit Adultery

You shall not Steal

Do not Bear False Witness

You shall not Covet

Meaning of Life

> [4] "Hear, O Israel: The Lord our God, the Lord is one! [5] You shall love the Lord your God with all your heart, with all your soul, and with all your strength.
>
> [6] "And these words which I command you today shall be in your heart. [7] You shall teach them diligently to your children, and shall talk of them when you sit in your house, when you walk by the way, when you lie down, and when you rise up.
>
> Deuteronomy - Chapter 6 Verses 4-7 (NKJV)

Promise Foretold

If you have broken these commandments, punishment is foretold, but there is a promised solution if you have sinned... *whether great or small.*

> [31] "Behold, the days are coming, says the Lord, when I will make a new covenant with the house of Israel and with the house of Judah— [32] not according to the covenant that I made with their fathers in the day that I took them by the hand to lead them out of the land of Egypt, My covenant which they broke, though I was a husband to them, says the Lord.
>
> [33] But this is the covenant that I will make with the house of Israel after those days, says the Lord: I will put My law in their minds, and write it on their hearts; and I will be their God, and they shall be My people.
>
> [34] No more shall every man teach his neighbor, and every man his brother, saying, 'Know the Lord,' for they all shall know Me, from the least of them to the greatest of them, says the Lord. For I will forgive their iniquity, and their sin I will remember no more."
>
> Jeremiah - Chapter 31 Verses 31 - 34 (NKJV)

The End of Days and Afterlife

...there shall be a time of trouble,
Such as never was since there was a nation,
Even to that time.
And at that time your people shall be delivered,
Every one who is found written in the book.
² And many of those who sleep in the dust of the earth shall awake,
Some to everlasting life,
Some to shame and everlasting contempt.
³ Those who are wise shall shine
Like the brightness of the firmament,
And those who turn many to righteousness
Like the stars forever and ever...

...¹³ "But [Daniel], go your way till the end; for you shall rest, and will arise to your inheritance at the end of the days."

Daniel - Chapter 12 Verses 1-3 & 13 (NKJV)

The PREDICTIONS Fulfilled
YESTERDAY AND TODAY

Show the final PREDICTIONS will be
FULFILLED TOMORROW

WHAT TO DO NOW

1) **Read the Scriptures.** There is so much more...

   Learn the Law - *it is right from wrong.*

   Learn the Predictions - *they are the proof for faith.*

   Learn the Character of God - *it is justice, love and mercy.*

2) **Join people who believe the Bible is the Word of God without equivocation.**

   The same God who accurately detailed the future of millions of lives, is the same God who inspired and preserved every verse of the rest of the Bible.

3) **Show others.** *Seeing is Believing.*

SHOW OTHERS - QUICKSHARE

At FORETOLD.COM everything we produce is made to share. Access free content, subscribe for expanded content, and purchase/download a host of products online...

QUICKSHARE - foretold.com/quickshare/

   Author Bob Jacobus takes you through an online tutorial that will make you a QuickShare hero in a matter of minutes.

FORETOLD.COM SUBSCRIPTION - Gain more than understanding, gain confidence to explain the predictions, the backgrounds, and the fulfillments - all to bring your friends and family to that eureka moment. *Seeing is Believing.*

Seeing is Believing!

QuickShare

Easy to See - Easy to Share

- Why
- Wow
- Nations
- Tyre
- Egypt
- Edom
- Date
- **Quick Share**

Foretold - Instructions

QuickShare

Quickly share the basics of Foretold by flipping through the predictions and pictures.

The headline to keep the prediction in mind as you view the images.

The prediction you are looking at will be highlighted.

Find the page number to Dig Deep in to the evidence in this booklet to answer difficult questions as you share!

Do Not Forget the WOW! Sum it all up and the evidence is beyond a reasonable doubt.

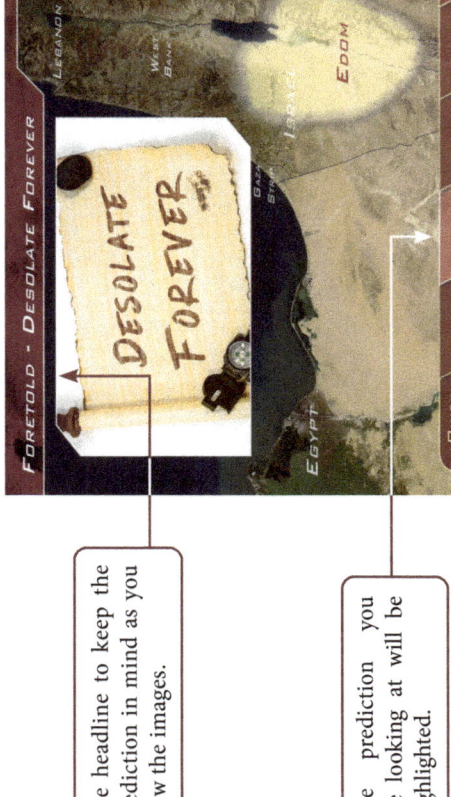

Quick Share > Date > Edom > Egypt > Tyre > Nations > Wow > Why

FORETOLD
Over 2,000 Years Ago

the Bible was found among the
DEAD SEA SCROLLS

THE BIBLE
Reference Edition

QUICK SHARE › DATE › EDOM › EGYPT › TYRE › NATIONS › WOW › WHY

Edom

Edomite dwellers
Approximated 800 - 200 BC

Foretold - Desolate Forever

PAGE 7

Syria
Iraq
Lebanon
Jordan
West Bank
Israel
Edom
Egypt

Desolate Forever

- Quick Share
- Date
- Edom
- Egypt
- Tyre
- Nations
- Wow
- Why

Edom

Foretold - Desolate Forever

PAGE 7

Quick Share | Date | Edom | Egypt | Tyre | Nations | Wow | Why

4.1

Edom
Desolate Forever

PAGE 7

Foretold - Desolate Forever

Quick Share | Date | Edom | Egypt | Tyre | Nations | Wow | Why

FORETOLD - TWO PART PREDICTION

EGYPT

Egypt border approximated 800 - 200 BC

Never Again Rule Nations

Forever the Lowliest of Kingdoms

Mediterranean Sea
Gaza Strip
West Bank
Israel
Jordan
Iraq
Ancient Egypt

PAGE 11

FORETOLD - NEVER RULE NATIONS AGAIN

EGYPT

CONQUERING EMPIRE
TO MINOR KINGDOM

QUICK SHARE | DATE | EDOM | EGYPT | TYRE | NATIONS | WOW | WHY

Egypt

In Shadow of Former Glory

A Third World Nation

Foretold - Forever Lowly

Quick Share | Date | Edom | Egypt | Tyre | Nations | Wow | Why

PAGE 17

FORETOLD - POWER TO FISHING TOWN

TYRE

Tyre Island and Mainland around 600 BC

- Lebanon
- Syria
- Tyre Mainland
- Israel
- Mediterranean Sea

Superpower to Fishing Town

| Quick Share | Date | Edom | Egypt | Tyre | Nations | Wow | Why |

TYRE

Foretold – Power to Fishing Town

PAGE 17

Quick Share › Date › Edom › Egypt › Tyre › Nations › Wow › Why

PAGE 26

FORETOLD - THE WOW

MILLIONS
OF LIVES

THOUSANDS
OF YEARS

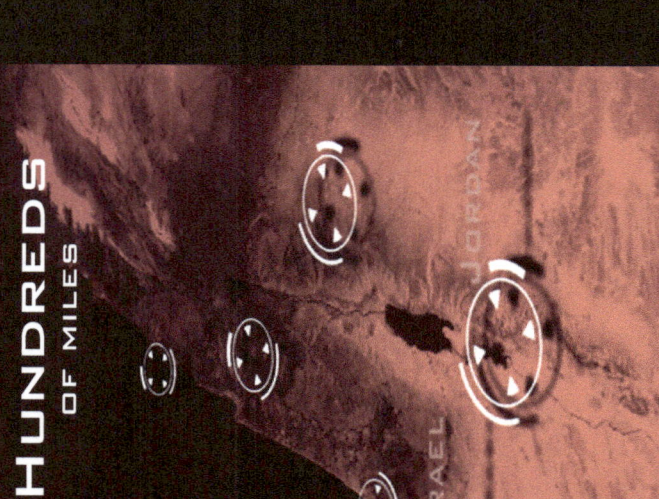

HUNDREDS
OF MILES

WHY
WOW
NATIONS
TYRE
EGYPT
EDOM
DATE
QUICK SHARE

The Why of Every Word

To teach -
Right From Wrong,
the Meaning of Life,
& Explain Your Future.

God Authenticates The Bible By Including History **BEFORE** *it Happens.*

| Quick Share | Date | Edom | Egypt | Tyre | Nations | Wow | Why |

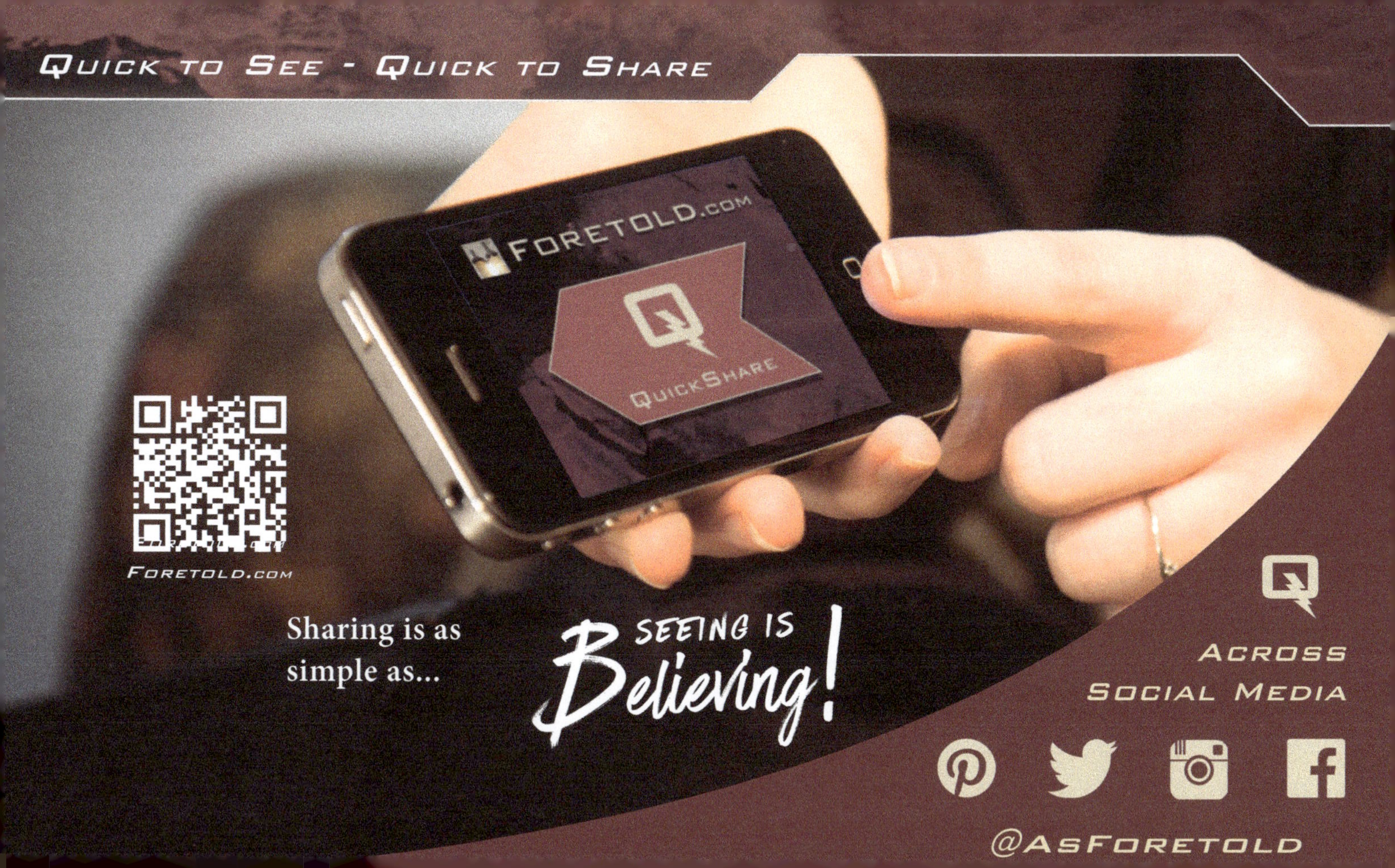

Quick to See - Quick to Share

Across Social Media

@asforetold

Seeing is Believing!

Sharing is as simple as...

Foretold.com

Endnotes

1. Comfort, Phillip Wesley, Editor, The Origin of the Bible, Wheaton, Il: Tyndale House, 1992, pp 153-154 *(from section four - an article contributed by Mark R. Norton, M.A.)*

2. Douglas, J.D., New Bible Dictionary, second edition, Wheaton: Tyndale House Publishers, Inc., 1982, p 1181.

3. Douglas, p 1182

4. Comfort, Philip Wesley, ed. The Origin of the Bible, Wheaton: Tyndale House Publishers, Inc., 1992, p 164

5. http://www.deadseascrolls.org.il/
   Author Note: Explore the actual fragments, the history of the discovery, and satellite & ground images of the source caves.

6. Chabries & Booras, The Petra Scrolls, ISPART, Brigham Young University, 2001, p 195. See also -https://acorjordan.org/the-petra-papyri/

7. Douglas, J.D., New Bible Dictionary, 2nd Edition, Wheaton, Il: Tyndale House, 1988, pp 301-303.

8. Douglas, p 307 & 1277

9. https://www.cia.gov/library/publications/resources/the-world-factbook/
   Author Note: 2017 CIA estimated figures

Tyre (pages 17-22) - General Sources (uncited but helpful)

Diodorus Siculus. Loeb Classic Library 8, ed. Charles H. Oldfather. Cambridge MA: Harvard University.

Herodotus, The Histories, trans. Aubrey De Sélincourt (London: Penguin).

Katzenstein, H. Jacob, The History of Tyre, second ed. Beersheba: Ben-Gurion University of the Negev

Hashim Sarkis Studios, "HOUSING for the FISHERMEN of TYRE, Lebanon", Architecture Lab, May 4, 2011, http://architecturelab.net/

10. Jidejian, Nina, Tyre Through the Ages, Beirut: Dar El-Mashreq Publishers, 1969, pp 52-141.
    Author Note: excellent survey of Tyre's history with a comprehensive bibliography upon which this record of conflict draws in part.

11. McDowell, Josh, Evidence That Demands A Verdict, Tyndale House Publishers, 1979, pp 297-298.

12. Payne, J. Barton, Encyclopedia of Biblical Prophecy, Grand Rapids, MI: Baker Books, 1973, pg 13.

For Further Reading (uncited but helpful)

Newman, Robert C., The Evidence of Prophecy, Hatfield, PA, Interdisciplinary Biblical Research Institute, 1988

Photo Credits

Front Cover - Art Design © 2018 Robert Jacobus,
    Edom - Monastery of Petra, Jordan, - ©2009 Alatom/iStock.com,
    Egypt - Giza, Pyramid - Tulay Over/iStock.com,
    Tyre - Old Harbor, Tyre-Lebanon - 2011 © dkaranouh/iStock.com

Pg 02 - NASA Visible Earth - Reto Stöckli, NASA Earth Observatory 2004 - Altered 2015 by Robert Jacobus

Pg 03 - Tied Scroll & Old Bible - © 2015 Robert Jacobus

Pg 04 - 05 - Holy Bible (left side bar) - © 2014 Robert Jacobus
Qumran settlement ruins, Judean Desert, Israel - ©2009 amit erez/iStock.com
Keter Aram Tzova, Aleppo Codex - circa 920 AD - Ardon Bar Hama - aleppocodex.org - published by the Custodial Committee (est. 1962) and the Ben Zvi Institute through Wiki Creative Commons Public Domain
Papyrus Rylands 458 - circa 2nd Century BC - 'Our Bible & the Ancient Manuscripts' by Sir Frederick Kenyon (1895 - 4th Ed. 1939) Pg 63 & Plate VI. - through Wiki Creative Commons Public Domain. Author Note: P458 presently housed at the University of Manchester's John Rylands Library

Pg 07 - Scroll Edom - © 2019 Robert Jacobus

Pg 08 - Amphitheater, Petra, Jordan - ©2010 CamPot/iStock.com

Pg 09 - Cave town Petra, Jordan - ©2010 CamPot/iStock.com

Pg 10 - Monastery of Petra, Jordan, - ©2009 Alatom/iStock.com

Pg 11 - Scrolls Egypt 1 & 2 - © 2019 Robert Jacobus

Pg 12 - Giza Pyramids, Cairo, Egypt - ©2008 Shishic/iStock.com

Pg 13 - Avenue of Ram-headed Sphinxes, Karnak Temples - ©2008 tenback/iStock.com

Pg 14 - Slum Cairo roofs with satellite dishes - ©2010 habari1/iStock.com

Pg 15 - Demonstrating for freedom - 2013 © Karim Mostafa/iStock.com
- *Description* Cairo, Egypt - November 21, 2011: People on Tahrir square are gathering around a protester. He and the rest of the crowd are demanding a stop of the military rule in Egypt.

Pg 16 - NASA Visible Earth - Reto Stöckli, NASA Earth Observatory 2004

Pg 17 - Scroll Tyre - © 2019 Robert Jacobus

Pg 18 - Old Harbor, Tyre-Lebanon - 2011 © dkaranouh/iStock.com

Pg 19 - Aerial View Tyre - October 26, 1938 (Original Photographer Unknown)

Pg 20 - Tyre Historical Map - © 2014 Robert Jacobus

Pg 21 - Ruins and architecture of Tyre, Lebanon - ©2012 benkrut/iStock.com
NASA-Lebanon_tmo_2011076_lrg-NASA image courtesy Jeff Schmaltz, MODIS Rapid Response Team at NASA GSFC

Pg 23 - Amphitheatre in city Amman, Jordan - 2012 © Daniel Smolcic/Dreamstime.com

Pg 24 - DVIDs - Nergal Gate in Nineveh, Iraq - Photo by Staff Sgt. JoAnn Makinano on Nov. 22, 2008. *The appearance of U.S. Department of Defense (DoD) visual information does not imply or constitute DoD endorsement.*

Pg 25 - Ruins of Ashdod on Mediterranean Sea - © Michael Egenburg/Shutterstock.com

Pg 26 - NASA Visible Earth - Reto Stöckli, NASA Earth 2004 (Altered/treatment by Robert Jacobus - 2018)
Hourglass - 2013 © LPETTET/iStock.com
Large crowd of people - 2017 5xinc/iStock.com

Pg 28 - Reading the Torah - 2012 © CrossEyedPhotography/iStock.com

Pg 29 - David Hume by Allan Ramsay, 1766 - Scottish National Portrait Gallery, Edinburgh - Public Domain
Carl Sagan - by Michael Okoniewski 1994 - Creative Commons Attribution 2.0 Generic license

Pg 30 - Scrolls © Dimdimich/Dreamstime.com

Pg 31 - Icons - © 2015 Robert Jacobus
NASA Visible Earth - Reto Stöckli, NASA Earth Observatory 2004

Pg 32 - Public Domain - Gustav Dore circa 1866

Pg 33 - 10 Commandments - © 2015 Robert Jacobus

Pg 35 - Old Bible © 2015 Robert Jacobus

Pg 36 - Share © 2014 Robert Jacobus

Pg 37 - NASA Visible Earth - Reto Stöckli, NASA Earth Observatory 2004 - Altered 2015 by Robert Jacobus

Pg 39 - Holy Bible (left side bar) - © 2014 Robert Jacobus
Qumran settlement ruins, Judean Desert, Israel - ©2009 amit erez/iStock.com

Pg 40 - NASA Visible Earth - Reto Stöckli, NASA Earth 2004
Inset Image - Scroll Edom - © 2014 Robert Jacobus

Pg 41 - Cave town Petra, Jordan - ©2010 CamPot/iStock.com
Inset Image - Amphitheater, Petra, Jordan - ©2010 CamPot/iStock.com

Pg 42 - Petra - the red city - © 2013 Hanis/iStock.com
Inset Image - Monastery of Petra, Jordan, - ©2009 Alatom/iStock.com

Pg 43 - NASA Visible Earth - Reto Stöckli, NASA Earth 2004
Inset Image - Scrolls Egypt 1 & 2 - © 2014 Robert Jacobus

Pg 44 - Pyramides of Giza - © 2007 sculpies/iStock.com
Inset Image - Demonstrating for freedom - 2013 © Karim Mostafa/iStock.com

Pg 45 - Cairo city skyline and Pyramids - © 2012 jethrostock/iStock.com
Inset Image - Slum Cairo roofs with satellite dishes - ©2010 habari1/iStock.com

Pg 46 - NASA Visible Earth - Reto Stöckli, NASA Earth 2004
Inset Image - Scroll Tyre - © 2019 Robert Jacobus

Pg 47 - Construction of boats in the port of the city of Tyre - © 2019 Marco Ramerini/iStockPhoto.com
Inset Image - Boats in the port of the city of Tyre - © 2019 Marco Ramerini/ iStockPhoto.com

Pg 48 - Old Harbor, Tyre-Lebanon - 2011 © dkaranouh/iStock.com

Pg 49 - Amphitheatre in city Amman, Jordan - 2012 © Daniel Smolcic/Dreamstime.com
DVIDs - Nergal Gate in Nineveh, Iraq - Photo by Staff Sgt. JoAnn Makinano on Nov. 22, 2008. *The appearance of U.S. Department of Defense (DoD) visual information does not imply or constitute DoD endorsement.*
Ruins of Ashdod on Mediterranean Sea - © Michael Egenburg/Shutterstock.com

Pg 50 - NASA Visible Earth - Reto Stöckli, NASA Earth 2004 (Altered/treatment by Robert Jacobus - 2018)
Hourglass - 2013 © LPETTET/iStock.com
Large crowd of people - 2017 5xinc/iStock.com

Pg 51 - Tied Scroll & Old Bible - © 2015 Robert Jacobus

Pg 52 - Share © 2014 Robert Jacobus

Back Cover - Map - CIA Worldbook. *Use of map image does not imply endorsement by the Central Intelligence Agency or any other governmental body of the United States.*
Image of Robert Jacobus © 2016 Robert Jacobus

Foretold.com   Digital Store

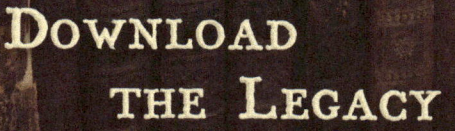

Download the Legacy
Foretold 1746

Foretold 1823

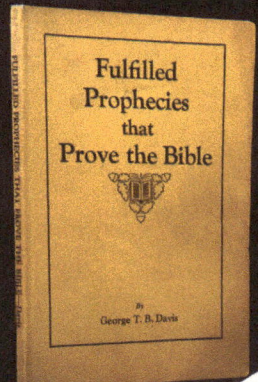

Foretold 1931

Digital Library of the Ages

Download the e-books   Foretold.com

FROM THE PRODUCER OF

1st Century Faith Engaging the 21st Century

FORETOLD.COM

 EXPERIENCE

> In seconds, end the debate.
>
> The evidence is beyond a reasonable doubt.
>
> - Bob Jacobus

THE AUTHOR

Bob Jacobus began his career in CBS and NBC news in Philadelphia, founded Mission Media to build and support a local association of 200 churches spanning over 40 denominations, and built media production companies serving Fortune 500 clients.

Bob has spoken in hundreds of churches, his media campaigns featured in national press, and presently focuses on simplifying the big ideas around the meaning of life and delivering the complex supporting evidence at a glance.

SPEAKER & DEBATES

Foretold presentations at Conferences, Events, Colleges, and Churches will take your audience around the world to experience the wonder of ancient empires today.

Our presentations are designed to reach secular and sacred audiences, always assuming the viewer is a skeptic.

Inquire online for future availabilities with Bob Jacobus or other team members.

FORETOLD.COM/SPEAKER